THE SECRETS OF EVERYDAY SAVINGS

Sylvain MILO N

CONTENTS

INTRODUCTION

The Secrets of Everyday Savings is a practical guide that will help you master the art of saving money in your everyday life. Whether you're looking to save money, pay down debt or improve your financial situation, this book will give you the tools you need to make significant savings without sacrificing your quality of life.

In today's society, where spending seems to be increasing all the time, it's essential to know how to manage your money effectively. However, many people feel overwhelmed and don't know where to start. The Secrets of Daily Savings offers a step-by-step action plan, with practical, easy-to-implement advice.

The book is divided into fifteen chapters, each tackling a specific aspect of everyday savings. From food budgets to energy bills, from online shopping to outings and leisure activities, you'll discover a wealth of tips and strategies for reducing your expenses and saving money.

Each chapter is designed to give you concrete advice and practical examples, enabling you to immediately apply the principles of thrift to your everyday life. Whether you're a student looking to save money on your snack budget or a parent with a large family trying to reduce monthly expenses, this book is for you.

Don't let money control your life. Take control of your finances and learn how to save money every day. The Secrets of Daily Savings will guide you on your journey to a more frugal life, while giving you the financial freedom and peace of mind you deserve.

CHAPTER 1: INTRODUCTION TO EVERYDAY SAVINGS

In this first chapter, we'll explore the importance of everyday savings and understand why it's essential to master this aspect of our financial lives. We'll also discover the benefits that saving can bring in the long term, and how to adopt a thrifty mentality on a daily basis.

The society we live in is ruled by consumerism and overspending. We are constantly bombarded by advertisements urging us to buy new products, try new experiences and spend our money without thinking. This frenetic consumer mentality can lead us to live beyond our means and accumulate debt.

That's why it's crucial to understand the importance of daily savings. Saving doesn't mean depriving yourself of all pleasure or living austerely. On the contrary, it means being aware of your spending, making informed decisions and spending your money wisely.

There are many long-term benefits to saving every day. Firstly, it allows us to build up an emergency fund. Having a reserve of money to deal with the unexpected, such as car repairs, medical expenses or job loss, gives us valuable peace of mind. What's more, savings can help us realize our long-term projects, such as buying a home, starting a business or planning our retirement.

By adopting a thrifty mentality on a daily basis, we also learn to value our money more. Instead of spending impulsively, we take the time to assess our real needs and find ways to save. This allows us to spend our money more thoughtfully and give more value to our purchases.

To start saving money on a daily basis, it's essential to become aware of our spending habits. Keep a spending diary for a week or a month to get an overview of your expenses. This will help you identify where you spend the most and where you could cut back.

Once you've identified your spending habits, you can start implementing money-saving strategies. For example, you can draw up a monthly budget and allocate a certain amount of money to each category of expenditure. This will enable you to better control your spending and identify areas where you can cut back.

Another effective strategy is to look for ways to save on your everyday expenses. For example, you can compare prices before you buy, use coupons or take advantage of promotional offers. What's more, you can consider cheaper alternatives for certain expenses, such as preparing meals at home instead of eating out.

Finally, it's important to remember that day-to-day savings aren't limited to expenses. You can also save by adopting energy-saving habits, such as reducing energy consumption, using public transport or recycling. These small actions can have a significant impact on your budget and the environment.

In conclusion, daily savings play an essential role in our financial lives. They enable us to live more responsibly, build a solid financial future and give more value to our money. By adopting a daily savings mentality, you'll be able to take control of your finances and achieve your long-term financial goals.

CHAPTER 2: REDUCING FOOD COSTS

Food is an unavoidable expense in our daily lives, but it can represent a significant part of our budget. In this chapter, we'll explore different strategies for reducing our food expenditure without compromising the quality of our food.

1. Meal planning: Meal planning is an essential step in reducing food costs. By planning the week's meals in advance, you can draw up a precise shopping list and avoid impulse purchases. It also helps avoid food waste, as you buy only what you need.

2. Make a shopping list: Before you head to the supermarket, take the time to draw up a shopping list based on your planned meals. This will help you avoid buying unnecessary products and keep you focused on the essentials. Try to stick to your list as much as possible to avoid impulse buying.

3. Compare prices: Don't just buy your food in one store. Take the time to compare prices in different stores, both online and in-store. You may be surprised at how much prices can vary from one place to another. Opt for promotions and discounts to save even more.

4. Choose seasonal produce: Seasonal produce is often cheaper and fresher. They are also more likely to be grown locally, which reduces the carbon footprint associated with transporting them. Find out what fruits, vegetables and seasonal produce are available in your area and incorporate them into your meals to save money while supporting local producers.

5. Cook at home: Eating out or buying ready-made meals can be expensive in the long run. Prefer home cooking, where you have control over the ingredients used and portion sizes. Cooking at home also allows you to prepare meals in large quantities, which you can freeze and consume at a later date, saving you time and money.

6. Avoid food waste: Food waste is not only a waste of money, but also a source of environmental damage. Learn to manage your leftovers creatively by incorporating them into new dishes. Use preservation techniques, such as canning or freezing, to extend the shelf life of your food. Also, be aware of expiration dates and use food before it spoils.

7. Buy in bulk: Whenever possible, opt to buy in bulk. This allows you to buy the exact quantity you need, reducing waste and the costs associated with packaging. Bring your own reusable containers to fill your bulk products, such as cereals, legumes and spices.

8. Grow a garden: If you have outdoor space, consider growing your own garden. Growing your own fruits, vegetables and herbs will cut your food costs considerably. What's more, it's a rewarding activity that connects you to nature and allows you to consume fresh, quality produce.

By applying these strategies, you can significantly reduce your food expenses while preserving the quality of your food. Think about your eating habits and adopt progressive changes to build a more economical and sustainable approach to food. Your wallet and your health will thank you.

CHAPTER 3: SAVING ON ENERGY BILLS

Energy bills can represent a significant proportion of our monthly expenses. In this chapter, we'll explore different strategies for reducing our energy costs and saving on our bills.

1. Home insulation: Home insulation is essential for reducing energy consumption. Make sure your home is properly insulated by checking windows, doors, walls and attics. Well-sealed windows and insulated doors can reduce heat loss in winter and keep the house cool in summer, reducing the need for excessive heating or air conditioning.

2. Efficient use of heating and cooling: Set your thermostat to a comfortable but economical temperature. By turning the heating down by one degree or the air conditioning up by one degree, you can make significant savings on your energy consumption. In addition, consider using programmable thermostats that allow you to automatically adjust the temperature to suit your schedule.

3. Energy-efficient lighting: Replace traditional light bulbs with more energy-efficient LED bulbs. LED bulbs consume up to 80% less energy than incandescent bulbs and last much longer. Also, turn off lights when you leave a room and use natural light as much as possible during the day.

4. Efficient use of appliances: Appliances can account for a significant proportion of a household's energy consumption. Choose energy-efficient appliances by opting for Energy Star-certified models. Use them efficiently, avoiding standby mode and unplugging them when not in use. Use low-temperature wash cycles for laundry and air-dry rather than tumble-dry.

5. Reduce hot water consumption: Hot water can account for a significant proportion of your energy bills. Reduce the temperature of your water heater to 50-55 degrees Celsius and use low-flow showers and faucets to save hot water. Fix water leaks too, as even a small leak can lead to a large loss of hot water and an increase in your bills.

6. Efficient use of electronic devices: Electronic devices can consume energy even in standby mode. Use power strips with switches to turn off your electronic devices completely when you're not using them. Also, avoid leaving your devices on charge once they are fully charged.

7. Responsible use of water and electricity: Adopt responsible habits when it comes to using water and electricity. Take shorter showers, use full dishwashers and washing machines, and turn off lights and appliances when you're not using them. These small gestures can have a significant impact on your energy bills.

By putting these strategies into practice, you can reduce your energy costs and save money on your bills. In addition to the financial benefits, you'll also be helping to preserve the environment by reducing your ecological footprint. Adopt these energy-saving habits in your daily life and you'll see a positive difference both on your bills and the environment.

CHAPTER 4: TIPS FOR SAVING MONEY WHEN SHOPPING ONLINE

Online shopping has become commonplace in our connected society. However, this doesn't mean we have to spend a fortune to get what we need. In this chapter, we're going to explore different ways of saving money when shopping online and maximizing our purchasing power.

1. Compare prices: One of the major advantages of online shopping is the ability to easily compare prices between different sellers. Before making a purchase, take the time to search for the same product on different websites and compare prices. Make sure you also take into account delivery costs and any available discount codes.

2. Use discount codes: Before finalizing your purchase, look for discount codes. Many websites offer promotional codes and coupons that you can use to get discounts on your online purchases. There are also browser extensions that can automatically search for and apply available discount codes during your purchasing process.

3. Take advantage of promotions and sales: Online shopping often offers special promotions and sales. Keep an eye on the websites of your favorite stores for current offers. Certain times of the year, such as Black Friday, Cyber Monday or the summer sales, are particularly good for big savings.

4. Subscribe to newsletters: Sign up for newsletters from e-commerce sites. Many retailers send exclusive offers and discount codes to their mailing list subscribers. This will keep you informed of promotions and new products, and ensure that you don't miss out on any special offers.

5. Use cashback sites: Cashback sites allow you to recoup part of the money you spend on your online purchases. Register with these platforms and use their affiliate links to make your purchases. You'll earn cashback that can be transferred to your bank account or used for future purchases.

6. Wait for sale periods: If you don't need an item immediately, consider waiting for sale periods to make your purchase. Online retailers often offer deep discounts during seasonal sales, which can help you save considerably on your purchases.

7. Read reviews and comments: Before buying a product online, take the time to read reviews and comments from other users. This will help you assess the quality of the product and make an informed decision. Also, beware of overly tempting offers or dubious websites. It's important to exercise caution and check the seller's reputation before making a purchase.

8. Avoid impulse buys: Online shopping can be tempting, but it's important to resist impulse buys. Take the time to think about

your real needs and the product's usefulness before adding it to your basket. Make a wish list and wait a few days before finalizing your purchase. This will allow you to take a step back and avoid unnecessary expenditure.

By putting these tips into practice, you can save considerably when shopping online. Don't forget to be vigilant, compare prices, look for discount codes and take advantage of special promotions. Online shopping can be a great bargain, as long as you're careful and strategic about your online transactions.

CHAPTER 5: REDUCING TRANSPORTATION COSTS

Transportation is an unavoidable expense in our lives, whether it's for getting to work, shopping or traveling. However, it is possible to reduce these expenses by adopting more economical habits and choices. In this chapter, we'll explore different strategies for reducing transportation-related expenses and saving money.

1. Use public transport: Public transport, such as buses, subways and trains, is often cheaper than private vehicles. Opt for public transport whenever possible, especially if you live in a well-served area. Monthly or annual season tickets can also offer additional discounts.

2. Share journeys: If you need to get to work or other destinations regularly, consider carpooling. Sharing journeys with colleagues or friends can split the cost of fuel and tolls. You can also find out about car-sharing platforms that match up drivers and passengers sharing the same route.

3. Opt for cycling or walking: For short journeys, opt for cycling

or walking. Not only will you save on fuel and parking costs, but you'll also improve your health by staying active. These eco-friendly and economical modes of transport are also ideal for journeys in city centers where traffic can be heavy.

4. Maintain your vehicle: If you own a car, make sure you keep it well maintained to minimize fuel and repair costs. Check tire pressure regularly, change the oil regularly and make sure the engine is in good condition. A well-maintained vehicle consumes less fuel and lasts longer.

5. Avoid traffic jams: Traffic jams can significantly increase fuel consumption and extend the duration of your journeys. Plan your journeys to avoid rush hours if possible, use navigation apps to find the fastest routes and consider alternatives, such as telecommuting, to reduce the number of car journeys.

6. Compare fuel prices: Fuel prices can vary from one service station to another. Before you fill up, check out the different service stations in your area to find the fuel at the best price. You can also use mobile applications or websites that show you fuel prices in real time.

7. Choose fuel-efficient vehicles: If you're thinking of buying a new vehicle, look into fuel-efficient models. Hybrids, electric vehicles or vehicles with more efficient diesel engines can help you save on fuel costs in the long term.

8. Use car-sharing services: If you only need a car once in a while, consider using car-sharing services such as car rental by the hour or day. This can be more economical than owning your own vehicle, as you only pay when you actually need it.

By putting these strategies into practice, you can significantly reduce your transportation expenses. Whether by opting for public transport, sharing journeys or choosing more economical modes of transport, every little change can have a significant impact on your budget. Be aware of your options and make smart choices to save money while getting around efficiently.

CHAPTER 6: SAVING ON OUTINGS AND LEISURE ACTIVITIES

Outings and leisure activities are an important part of our social life, but they can also take a heavy toll on our budget. In this chapter, we'll explore a number of tips on how to save money on outings and leisure activities, while still enjoying pleasant and entertaining moments.

1. Look for special offers: Before planning an outing or leisure activity, find out what special offers and discounts are available. Many websites offer promotional offers, coupons or packages that can save you money on entrance tickets, meals or activities. Take the time to compare prices and choose the most advantageous option.

2. Take advantage of reduced rates: Many entertainment venues, such as museums, cinemas or theme parks, offer reduced rates at certain times of the day or to specific groups (students, senior citizens, families, etc.). Find out more about these offers and plan your outings accordingly to benefit from lower rates.

3. Organize free or low-cost outings: There are many free or

low-cost leisure activities. Organize outdoor outings, picnics, hikes or visits to historical or cultural sites. Explore local parks, attend community events or participate in free workshops. These activities will allow you to spend quality time without spending a lot of money.

4. Subscriptions and passes: If you plan to visit an entertainment venue regularly, consider taking out a subscription or buying a pass. Many theaters, sports clubs, leisure centers and museums offer monthly or annual subscriptions or passes that offer reduced rates or unlimited access to certain activities. Do the math to determine whether these options are worthwhile for your intended use.

5. Organize evenings at home: Going out can be expensive, especially when you add the expense of food and drink. Organize evenings at home by inviting friends or relatives over for board games, film screenings, shared meals or barbecues. Not only does this cut costs, but it also creates a friendly, intimate environment.

6. Use booking apps and websites: Many booking apps and websites offer discounted rates or special offers on restaurants, leisure activities, shows and events. Use these tools to find the best deals available in your area and save on your outings.

7. Find affordable hobbies that match your interests. Opt for free or low-cost activities such as reading, gardening, DIY, home yoga or cooking. Also explore online resources, such as tutorials or free courses, to discover new activities without spending a lot of money.

8. Set a budget for outings and leisure activities: Set yourself a monthly budget for outings and leisure activities and stick to

it. This will help you control your spending and make more informed decisions. You can also set aside part of your budget for special activities or events that you particularly want to experience.

By putting these tips into practice, you can enjoy outings and leisure activities while keeping your expenses under control. Look for special offers, opt for free or low-cost activities, organize outings at home and set a budget to keep your leisure spending under control. Remember, it's possible to enjoy yourself without emptying your wallet - you just have to be creative and explore all the options available.

CHAPTER 7: MANAGING YOUR BUDGET EFFECTIVELY

Effective budget management is essential to achieving your financial goals and ensuring your financial stability. In this chapter, we'll explore different strategies for managing your budget effectively and optimizing your spending.

1. Take stock of your income and expenses: The first step in budget management is to get a clear picture of your income and expenses. Take the time to assess your monthly income, including salaries, supplementary income and other sources of income. Next, examine your expenses in detail, categorizing fixed expenses (rent, bills, etc.) and variable expenses (food, entertainment, etc.). This assessment will help you identify where your money is going and make informed decisions to optimize your budget.

2. Draw up a realistic budget: Use the information you've gathered to draw up a realistic budget. Allocate a portion of your income to each expense category, including savings. Set clear financial goals, such as paying off debt, saving for a major purchase or building an emergency fund, and include them in your budget. Make sure your expenses don't exceed your income, and adjust if necessary to achieve a financial balance.

3. Track your expenses: Keep regular track of your expenses to make sure you stay within your budget. You can do this by using expense-tracking apps, recording your spending in a diary or using spreadsheets. The aim is to know where your money is going, detect areas where you could cut back and keep track of your progress towards your financial goals.

4. Prioritize savings: Savings are a crucial part of budget management. Set yourself a monthly savings target and include it in your budget from the outset. Make saving a priority, just like paying your other bills. Automate your savings by setting up automatic transfers to a savings account each month. This will help you build up a financial reserve and prepare for the unexpected.

5. Reduce unnecessary expenses: Analyze your expenses and identify areas where you could reduce unnecessary spending. This could include unused subscriptions, impulse spending or excessive consumer habits. Identify these areas and take steps to reduce or eliminate them. For example, you could cancel certain subscriptions, switch to cheaper alternatives or practice more conscious consumption.

6. Negotiate bills and contracts: Don't underestimate the power of negotiation. Contact your service providers (internet, telephone, insurance, etc.) to assess whether you can get better rates or promotional offers. Also explore competing offers and use them as leverage to negotiate with your current supplier. Negotiating can save you a lot of money on your monthly bills.

7. Anticipate future expenses: Anticipate future expenses such as car maintenance, home repairs or vacation expenses. Including these expenses in your budget will allow you to set money aside in

advance and not be caught unprepared when these expenses arise. You can set up a separate fund for these long-term expenses.

8. Review your budget regularly: Budget management is an ongoing process. Review your budget regularly, assess your progress and make any necessary adjustments. Your financial situation may change, new goals may emerge and certain expenses may vary. Be flexible and adapt your budget accordingly to stay in control of your finances.

By putting these strategies into practice, you'll be able to effectively manage your budget and optimize your spending. Budget management helps you take control of your finances, achieve your financial goals and live a more financially secure life. Be diligent, follow your budget and adjust it according to your needs and goals.

CHAPTER 8: SAVING ON BEAUTY AND HYGIENE PRODUCTS

Beauty and hygiene products can account for a significant proportion of our monthly expenses. However, it is possible to reduce these expenses by adopting intelligent and economical strategies. In this chapter, we'll explore different ways of saving on beauty and hygiene products while taking care of yourself.

1. Make a list of necessary products: Before buying beauty and hygiene products, make a list of the items you really need. Avoid impulse purchases and concentrate on the essentials. By having a clear list, you'll avoid buying unnecessary products and you'll be able to better control your spending.

2. Compare prices: Don't just buy from one store. Take the time to compare prices in different physical stores and online. You may find significant price differences for the same products. Don't hesitate to take advantage of promotional offers and discounts to save even more.

3. Opt for affordable brands: Beauty and personal care brands often offer affordable alternatives without compromising quality.

Do your research and identify brands that offer quality products at more affordable prices. You can also consult online reviews and comments to get an idea of product performance before you buy.

4. Choose multi-purpose products: Choose products that have several uses. For example, opt for a facial cleanser that can also be used as a make-up remover, or a lip balm that can be used as a cuticle moisturizer. By using multi-use products, you'll reduce the number of products you need to buy and save money.

5. Use samples and travel sizes: Take advantage of the free samples or travel sizes offered by brands. This will enable you to test the products before buying them in full size. What's more, travel sizes are less expensive than full versions and are ideal for travel or temporary use.

6. Make certain products yourself: You can save money by making certain beauty and hygiene products yourself. For example, you can create your own body scrub by mixing sugar and olive oil, or make a nourishing hair mask from natural ingredients. There are many recipes and tutorials online to guide you in creating your own products.

7. Use promotions and sales: Watch out for promotions and sales to take advantage of discounts on beauty and hygiene products. Many stores and websites offer special deals, such as "buy one, get one free" or deep discounts. Plan your purchases accordingly to take advantage of these attractive offers.

8. Stretch products to the last drop: Use products until they're completely exhausted. For example, cut up toothpaste tubes to extract every last portion, or dilute leftover shampoo to make a final wash. By using products to the last drop, you'll maximize

their use and extend their lifespan, so you won't have to repurchase them frequently.

By putting these tips into practice, you can save money on your beauty and hygiene expenses. Be aware of your real needs, compare prices, opt for affordable brands and take advantage of promotions. Don't hesitate to get creative and make some products yourself. With these strategies, you'll be able to take care of yourself on a budget.

CHAPTER 9: SAVING MONEY WHILE TRAVELING

Traveling can be a wonderful experience, but that doesn't mean you have to spend a fortune exploring new places. In this chapter, we'll explore different tips for saving money when traveling and enjoying affordable vacations.

1. Plan ahead: One of the keys to saving money when traveling is to plan ahead. Book your air tickets and accommodation several months in advance to take advantage of the lowest fares. What's more, by planning ahead, you have time to search for the best deals and compare prices for every aspect of your trip.

2. Travel during low season: Prices for flights, hotels and tourist attractions can vary considerably depending on the season. Traveling during the off-season allows you to take advantage of lower fares and avoid the crowds of tourists. In addition to saving money, you'll enjoy a more authentic travel experience.

3. Use flight and hotel comparators: Use comparison websites and apps to find the cheapest flights and accommodation. These tools let you compare prices from different airlines and hotels in one

place, saving you time and money. Don't forget to check traveler reviews and comments to make sure you're getting the best value for money.

4. Opt for budget accommodation: Opt for budget accommodation such as youth hostels, bed & breakfasts or vacation rentals. These options are often less expensive than larger hotels, while offering a more authentic and friendly experience. You could also consider couchsurfing, a practice where travelers are hosted free of charge by locals.

5. Explore local transportation options: Instead of taking cabs or renting a car, explore local transportation options. Use public transport, such as buses, subways or trains, which are often much cheaper. You can also opt to rent a bike or walk to explore local destinations, which will also allow you to discover the city in a more immersive way.

6. Eat locally: Avoid expensive tourist restaurants and go for places frequented by locals. Eating in local restaurants or even buying food in markets and grocery stores can be much cheaper. This will also give you the chance to discover local cuisine and interact with the locals.

7. Take advantage of free or low-cost activities: Find out what free or low-cost activities are available in your destination. Many cities offer free guided tours, free museums on certain days of the week or cultural or artistic events accessible to all. Check local calendars and search online for low-cost entertainment options.

8. Limit expensive souvenirs: Souvenirs can quickly become a major expense during a trip. Limit impulse purchases of expensive souvenirs and opt for more affordable ones such as

postcards, magnets or local handicrafts. You can also choose to take photos to immortalize your experiences without spending any money.

By putting these tips into practice, you can make significant savings when traveling. Plan ahead, compare prices, travel in low season and use economical accommodation and transport. Explore local options, take advantage of free activities and limit overspending. Remember, travel isn't just about the destination, it's about the experience.

CHAPTER 10: SAVING ON CLOTHES AND FASHION

Fashion may be a passion for some, but that doesn't mean you have to spend a fortune to keep up with the latest trends. In this chapter, we'll explore different tips for saving money on clothes and fashion while staying stylish.

1. Make an inventory of your wardrobe: Before making any purchases, make an inventory of your wardrobe. Identify the pieces you already own and assess their condition and versatility. This will help you better understand what you really need and avoid buying similar or unnecessary items.

2. Choose quality over quantity: Opt for quality clothes rather than cheap items that wear out quickly. Even if it means spending a little more up front, quality clothing will last longer and save you money in the long run. Look for brands with a reputation for durability and quality workmanship.

3. Take advantage of sales and promotions: Watch out for sales and promotions to get clothes at reduced prices. Stores often offer big discounts during seasonal sales periods. You can also sign up

for brand newsletters to keep up to date with special offers and discount codes.

4. Buy second-hand: Second-hand clothes are a great way to save on fashion expenses. Explore thrift stores, second-hand stores or second-hand clothing websites. You can find unique, quality pieces at considerably reduced prices. Be sure to inspect clothing carefully to ensure it's in good condition.

5. Swap or borrow clothes: Organize clothing swaps with friends, family or even colleagues. You can also consider borrowing clothes for special occasions rather than buying new outfits. This will allow you to diversify your wardrobe without spending extra money.

6. Learn to make alterations: If you have basic sewing skills, you can save money by making your own alterations. Learn how to shorten pants, adjust dresses or replace buttons. This way, you can give new life to your existing clothes instead of buying new ones.

7. Focus on timeless basics: Invest in timeless basics such as quality jeans, white shirts, black blazers and so on. These versatile pieces can be easily combined with other items in your wardrobe, allowing you to create different looks without having to buy new outfits every time.

8. Follow trends sparingly: Don't give in to every passing trend. Choose wisely the trends you wish to adhere to and buy only a few key pieces to complete your wardrobe. This will prevent you from spending money on items that will quickly become obsolete.

9. Take care of your clothes: Take good care of your clothes to prolong their life. Follow washing instructions, store them

properly and repair them as soon as necessary. The better you look after your clothes, the less frequently you'll have to buy new ones.

By putting these tips into practice, you can save money on clothes and fashion while staying ahead of the trends. Take stock of your wardrobe, focus on quality, take advantage of sales, explore second-hand clothes and learn how to make alterations. Don't forget to choose timeless basics and take good care of your clothes to make them last longer.

CHAPTER 11: REDUCING SPENDING ON HEALTH AND MEDICAL CARE

Health is a priority, but that doesn't mean you have to spend a fortune to keep yourself in good shape and access quality medical care. In this chapter, we'll explore a number of tips for reducing health and medical expenses while preserving your well-being.

1. Prevent health problems: Adopt a healthy lifestyle to prevent health problems and reduce long-term medical expenses. Maintain a balanced diet, exercise regularly, avoid smoking and limit alcohol consumption. By taking care of your health, you can avoid many costly health problems.

2. Get regular check-ups: Prevention is key to detecting health problems at an early stage. Get regular check-ups, such as blood tests, dental examinations and health screenings, to identify any potential health problems. By detecting health problems at an early stage, you can avoid costly long-term complications.

3. Compare healthcare professionals' prices: When you need to

consult a healthcare professional, take the time to compare prices. Prices can vary from one professional to another, even for the same medical services. Look for reviews and recommendations, then compare rates to find an affordable, quality healthcare professional.

4. Use free or low-cost health services: Find out what free or low-cost health services are available in your area. Many governments offer public health programs that provide medical services at reduced or free rates. You can also explore community clinics, local health centers or medical assistance programs to find affordable medical care.

5. Get the right health insurance: If you don't already have health insurance, explore the different options available and choose one that suits your needs. Compare policies to find affordable coverage that meets your medical needs. Make sure you understand the conditions, limits and exclusions of your insurance to avoid financial surprises.

6. Use generic drugs: When you need medication, ask your doctor or pharmacist if generic versions are available. Generic medications are less expensive alternatives to brand-name drugs, but they contain the same active ingredients and are just as effective. By choosing generic drugs, you can make significant savings on your drug costs.

7. Research drug costs: Before buying drugs, research the different suppliers and compare prices. You may find significant price variations from one pharmacy to another. Don't hesitate to ask your doctor or pharmacist about the most affordable options.

8. Find out about financial assistance programs: Certain expensive

drugs or specific treatments may be eligible for financial assistance programs. Check with drug manufacturers or health organizations to find out if you are eligible for cost reduction or financial assistance programs.

By putting these tips into practice, you can reduce your health and medical expenses while preserving your well-being. Prevent health problems, have regular check-ups, compare the prices of healthcare professionals and use free or low-cost healthcare services. Take out appropriate health insurance, opt for generic drugs, research drug costs and find out about financial assistance programs. Managing your health responsibly can help you save money and ensure a healthy future.

CHAPTER 12: SAVING ON HOME MAINTENANCE

Home maintenance is an unavoidable task, but that doesn't mean you have to spend a fortune to keep your home in good condition. In this chapter, we'll explore different tips for saving money on home maintenance and reducing your expenses.

1. Plan maintenance tasks: Make a calendar of your home maintenance tasks and plan them in advance. This will help you stay organized, avoid forgetting important tasks and prevent potential problems. Regular maintenance will help you avoid costly repairs in the long run.

2. Do-it-yourself repairs: Learn how to carry out certain repairs and small jobs around the house yourself. Many online resources offer tutorials and guides to guide you through common repairs. By doing the repairs yourself, you'll save on labor costs.

3. Use homemade cleaning products: Avoid buying expensive cleaning products by opting for homemade alternatives. For example, you can use white vinegar and baking soda to clean surfaces, lemon to remove stains and Marseille soap for laundry.

These products are economical, environmentally friendly and just as effective.

4. Save on energy: Reduce your energy costs by adopting energy-saving habits. Turn off the lights when you leave a room, use energy-saving light bulbs, program your thermostat to regulate the temperature and unplug electronic devices when not in use. These small actions can significantly reduce your energy bills.

5. Maintain appliances regularly: Maintain your appliances regularly to extend their life and avoid costly repairs. Clean the filters on your range hood, defrost your refrigerator regularly, clean the vents on your tumble dryer and perform regular maintenance on your air conditioning and heating systems.

6. Reuse and recycle: Give objects a second life rather than throwing them away. Reuse glass jars for storage, turn old clothes into cleaning rags and recycle materials such as cardboard, glass and plastic. By recycling and reusing, you'll reduce the cost of buying new products.

7. Buy supplies in bulk: Save on cleaning products by buying supplies in bulk. Buy products in large quantities, such as toilet paper, cleaning products or garbage bags, to get discounted prices per unit. Make sure you store these supplies properly, so they stay in good condition until you use them.

8. Use local professionals: When you need professional maintenance services, give preference to local companies. Not only does this support the local economy, but it can also get you competitive rates. Ask for recommendations and compare prices to find reliable, affordable professionals.

By putting these tips into practice, you can save money on home maintenance while preserving its quality and value. Plan maintenance tasks, do some repairs yourself, use homemade cleaning products and adopt energy-saving habits. Maintain your appliances regularly, reuse and recycle, buy supplies in bulk and call in local professionals when necessary. By taking care of your home economically, you'll save money in the long run while maintaining a clean, comfortable environment.

CHAPTER 13: TIPS FOR SAVING ON GIFTS AND SPECIAL OCCASIONS

Gifts and special occasions can be joyous occasions, but that doesn't mean you have to spend a fortune to show your affection and celebrate with your loved ones. In this chapter, we'll explore different tips for saving money on gifts and special occasions while preserving their meaning and value.

1. Set a budget: Before making purchases for gifts or special occasions, establish a clear budget. Determine how much you're willing to spend on each occasion, and stick to that budget. This will help you make informed decisions and avoid overspending.

2. Give homemade gifts: Homemade gifts have sentimental value and can be much appreciated. Use your skills and creativity to create unique gifts such as personalized photo albums, homemade cookies, crafts or poems. Homemade gifts are often less expensive than store-bought gifts, but have much greater personal value.

3. Organize gift exchanges: Instead of buying gifts for each person on special occasions with family or friends, organize gift

exchanges. Set a maximum budget for gifts, and draw the names of the people to whom you will give gifts. This reduces the number of gifts to buy, while preserving the spirit of generosity and celebration.

4. Shop ahead: Anticipate special occasions and birthdays by shopping ahead. When you come across a good deal or the perfect gift for someone, buy it and save it for the appropriate occasion. This will save you money and prevent you from spending hastily at the last minute.

5. Use coupon sites and promo codes: Check out websites specializing in coupons and promo codes to find great deals on gifts and festive items. Many sites offer exclusive discounts, promo codes or flash sales that allow you to buy gifts at reduced prices. Take the time to research and compare prices before making your purchase.

6. Offer experiences rather than objects: Instead of buying material gifts, consider offering memorable experiences. Offer vouchers for activities such as dinner out, a day at the spa, a cultural outing or a weekend getaway. Experiences offer precious moments and can be less expensive than buying physical gifts.

7. Reuse and recycle gift wrap: Don't waste money on expensive, short-lived gift wrap. Reuse gift wrapping you already have, or recycle materials such as newspapers, magazines or fabric scraps to create your own unique, personalized wrapping.

8. Communicate and share your intentions: If you want to cut back on spending on gifts and special occasions, communicate with your loved ones and share your intentions. Explain that you're looking to save money and suggest alternatives such as

exchanging services, spending quality time together or symbolic gifts. The important thing is to celebrate special moments and show your affection, no matter how expensive the gifts.

By putting these tips into practice, you can save money on gifts and special occasions while preserving their meaning and significance. Set a budget, give homemade gifts, organize gift exchanges and shop in advance. Use good deals sites, offer experiences, reuse gift wrapping and communicate with your loved ones. Remember that intention and gesture are more important than the cost of a gift, and that special occasions can be celebrated in a meaningful and cost-effective way.

CHAPTER 14: SAVING FOR THE FUTURE: SAVINGS AND INVESTMENT TIPS

Saving and investing are key to your long-term financial security. In this chapter, we'll explore various tips and tricks to help you save for the future and make informed savings and investment decisions.

1. Set financial goals: Start by defining your long-term financial objectives. Whether it's buying a house, building an emergency fund or preparing for retirement, clear goals will help you stay motivated and guide your financial decisions.

2. Establish a budget: A well-established budget is the key to saving money. Review your monthly income and expenses, and identify areas where you can cut back. Set limits on discretionary spending, and allocate a portion of your income to savings and investment.

3. Create an emergency fund: Set up an emergency fund to cover unexpected expenses such as medical bills, home repairs or job

loss. Aim to save enough to cover at least three to six months of living expenses. Place this fund in a liquid, easily accessible savings account.

4. Automate your savings: Set up automatic transfers to transfer a portion of your income to a savings account each month. This will help you save regularly without extra effort. Treat your savings as an essential, priority expense.

5. Reduce debt: Eliminate high-interest debt as quickly as possible. Concentrate on paying off high-interest credit cards, personal loans or student loans. Less debt means less interest to pay, which will save you more money in the long run.

6. Diversify your investments: When you're ready to invest, diversify your portfolio. Don't put all your savings into one type of investment. Invest in different sectors, asset classes and geographic regions to reduce risk and maximize return opportunities.

7. Explore investment options: Learn about different investment options such as stocks, bonds, mutual funds, index funds, ETFs and real estate. Consult a financial advisor or do your own research to understand the benefits and risks of each option and choose those that match your objectives and risk profile.

8. Consult a financial advisor: If you need help establishing a solid financial plan, consider consulting a qualified financial advisor. An advisor can help you define your goals, develop a savings and investment strategy, and adjust your plan based on your personal situation.

9. Take advantage of tax benefits: Find out about the tax

advantages of saving and investing, such as individual retirement plans (RRSPs) or tax-free savings accounts (TFSAs). These accounts offer tax advantages that can help you increase your savings over the long term.

10. Follow up regularly: Review your savings and investment progress regularly. Reassess your goals, adjust your plan if necessary, and make sure your investments are in line with your objectives and risk tolerance.

By following these savings and investment tips, you can put in place a solid financial strategy for the future. Set goals, create a budget, build an emergency fund and automate your savings. Reduce your debts, diversify your investments, explore investment options and consult a financial advisor if necessary. Take advantage of tax benefits and monitor your progress regularly. With a thoughtful, proactive approach, you can make the right financial decisions to secure your financial future.

CHAPTER 15: CONCLUSION - ADOPTING A THRIFTY MENTALITY ON A DAILY BASIS

Congratulations! You've read this book, which is full of tips and advice on how to save money every day. You now have the knowledge you need to adopt a thrifty mentality that will enable you to better manage your finances, achieve your financial goals and live more consciously.

Everyday economy doesn't mean depriving ourselves of everything, but rather making informed decisions to spend our money wisely and maximize our resources. This means rethinking our consumption habits, looking for economical alternatives and being creative to save money without sacrificing our quality of life.

Over the course of the chapters, we've explored different facets of everyday saving, from reducing food expenses to effective budget management, energy savings, online shopping, transportation expenses, leisure, beauty care, travel, clothing, health, gifts and investments. You'll learn how to spot savings opportunities, make informed decisions and apply simple money-saving tips to all aspects of your life.

Adopting a thrifty mentality on a daily basis will bring you many benefits. First of all, it will help you improve your financial situation by reducing your spending and saving more. It will also free you from financial stress, help you achieve your short- and long-term financial goals, and create a solid plan for your financial future.

By adopting a thrifty mentality, you also develop a heightened awareness of the value of money and how you choose to spend it. You become more aware of your consumption habits, of your real needs versus your desires, and of the impact of your financial choices on your life and on the environment.

However, it's important to note that day-to-day saving doesn't have to become an obsession. It's important to strike a balance between managing your finances and your overall well-being. It's perfectly acceptable to indulge in occasional pleasures and enjoy life, as long as you do so thoughtfully and with consideration for your financial situation.

Remember, too, that saving money on a daily basis is not an isolated task, but rather a way of life. It's an ongoing process that requires discipline, patience and perseverance. Continue to educate yourself, seek out new money-saving tips and adapt your approach according to your personal evolution and goals.

In conclusion, adopting a thrifty mindset on a daily basis is a powerful choice that can have a significant impact on your financial life and overall well-being. By putting the advice in this book into practice,

you're well on your way to living a more conscious, economical and fulfilling life. So don't wait any longer, take control of your finances and build a financially secure and balanced future. Good luck on your journey towards a life of everyday thrift!